T0193614

Spot the Spot

with Maren and Ivy

Lindsay Ann Fink

Balboa Press books may be ordered through booksellers or by contacting:

Balboa Press
A Division of Hay House
1663 Liberty Drive
Bloomington, IN 47403
www.balboapress.com
844-682-1282

ISBN: 979-8-7652-2734-3 (sc)
ISBN: 979-8-7652-5136-2 (hc)
ISBN: 979-8-7652-2735-0 (e)

Print information available on the last page.

Balboa Press rev. date: 04/15/2024

BALBOA.PRESS

Spot the Spot

with
Maren and Ivy

Lindsay Ann Fink

This is a game that is super fun to play. It's called Spot the Spot. Maren and Ivy have the wildest imaginations; they are more creative than a playstation. Maren is a clever one; she has the best ideas that are super fun. Ivy is the sporty one; she can easily make up a game to be played outside in the sun.

Maren or Ivy will give a clue then you have to guess the color of the spot, go find it and then use your imagination.

First Maren says I have a color in mind.

The clue is at the traffic light

it means we have to stop.

Can you guess it?

Is it red?

Great run to the red spot and

hop, hop, hop,

three times, then stop.

Ivy's turn. Ivy says This is a color that is a tasty fruit, it's round and grows on a tree.

Can you guess it?

Is it an orange?

Well done, go find the orange one.

Now pick it up and pretend to drive around like you are in a race car.

Vroom vroom

Maren is thinking about her color next.
She takes the yellow spot and
places it on the board she draws some
rays and turns it into the golden sun.
Go find a yellow spot and make a
big golden sun.

Ivy says her next color rhymes with bean.

Can you guess it?

Is it the color green?

Good job green beans let's take our green spot and pretend we are a growing green bean starting small like a teeny tiny bean.

Then slowly stretch your leaves out.

Reach your stem up towards the yellow sun and stand tall like a giant green bean sprout.

Maren has a color in mind; it is the same color as the sky and the water.
Can you guess it?
Blue is the color for you.
Can you spot the blue spot?
Find the blue spot and show me how you swim in the blue sea.
Well done, this is fun.
Let's find another one.

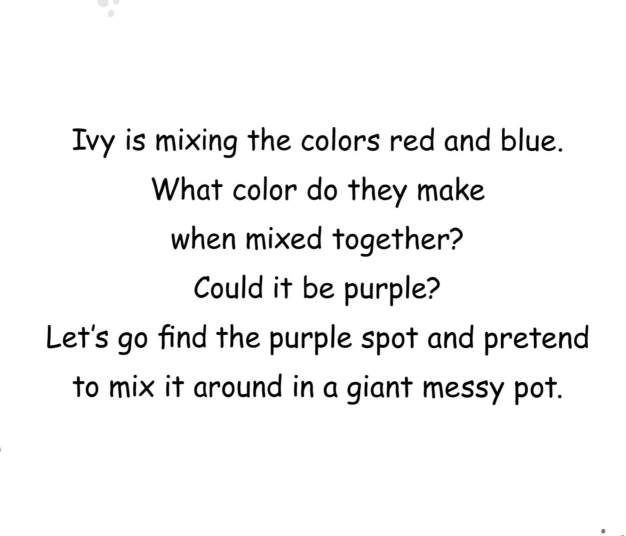

Ivy is mixing the colors red and blue.
What color do they make
when mixed together?
Could it be purple?
Let's go find the purple spot and pretend
to mix it around in a giant messy pot.

Maren says I have a spot in mind.

It's the color of a beautiful bird

and the color rhymes with sink.

You guessed it -it is pink.

Flap your wings over to the pink spot

just like the pink flamingo.

Can you balance there on the pink

spot like a flamingo on one leg.

Now can you reach down and try to eat

the pink shrimp in the water,

they are secret to how the flamingo

gets to be so pink..

Ivy is ready to find the spot the same color as the clouds.
Can you guess what the color is?
White well you are right about that.
Find the white spot and lay down like you are a cloud floating around.

Maren looks down and says she has

a color that rhymes with ground.

Can you guess it?

It's the color brown.

Find the brown spot and imagine you

are burying a treasure digging

a giant hole in the ground

The girls are getting tired. It's almost nighttime.
What color does the sky turn at night?
Black is right. Can you spot the black spot
and lay down to say goodnight?

Good night sleepy one, let's play this game
again in the morning's sun.

Can you make a Spot and color it any color you want?

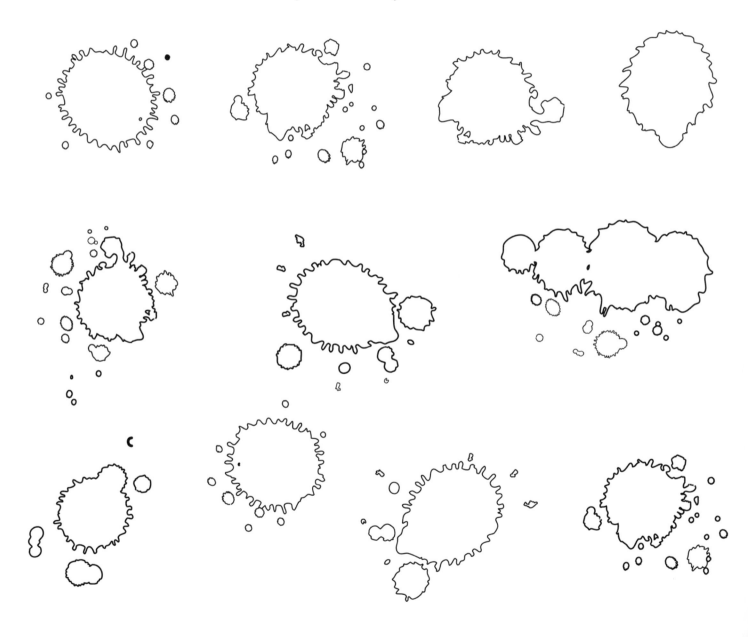

Printed in the United States
by Baker & Taylor Publisher Services